SCHIRMER
PERFORMANCE
EDITIONS

LABORUM
DULCE
LENIMEN

G. SCHIRMER

RACHMANINOFF

T0082020

PRELUDES
Opus 32

Edited and Recorded by Alexandre Dossin

On the cover:
Die Heimkehr, (1887)
by Arnold Böcklin
(1827–1901)

ISBN 978-1-4786-1279-3

G. SCHIRMER, Inc.

DISTRIBUTED BY

HAL•LEONARD®
CORPORATION

7777 W. BLUEMOUND RD. P.O. BOX 13819 MILWAUKEE, WI 53213

www.musicsalesclassical.com
www.halleonard.com

CONTENTS

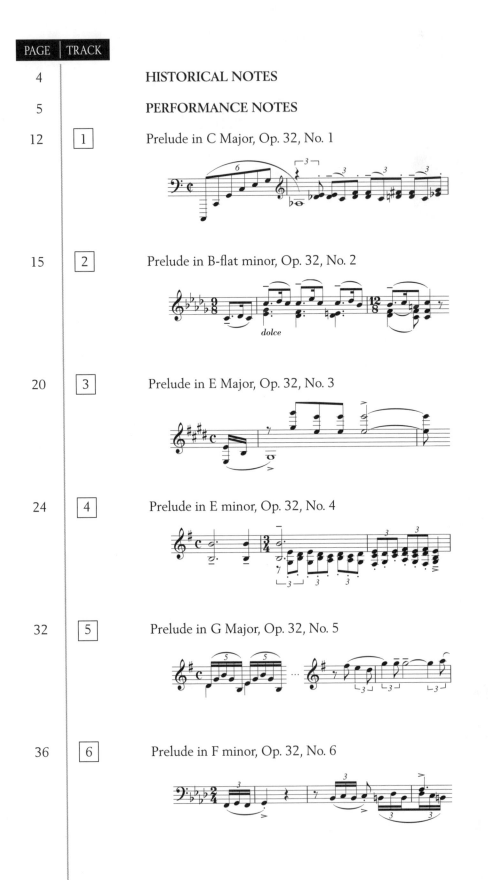

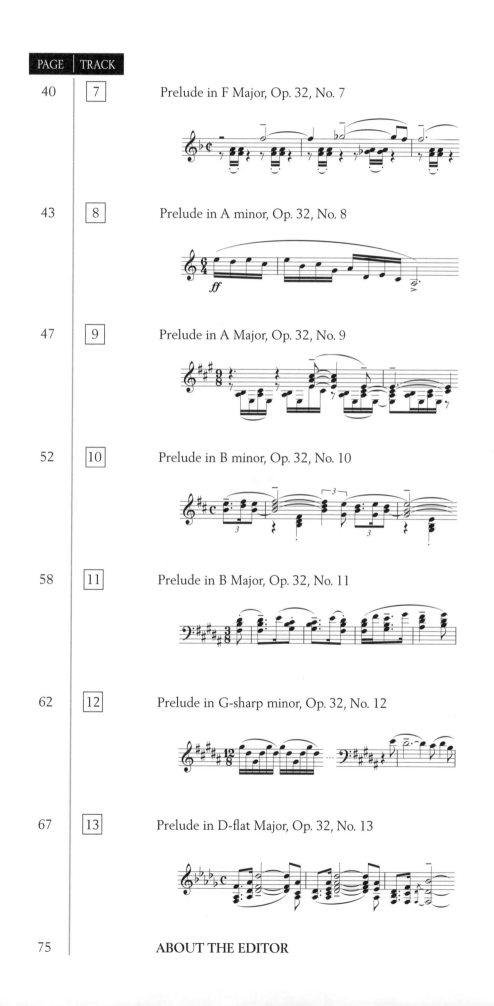

HISTORICAL NOTES

Sergei Rachmaninoff (1873–1943)

Sergei Rachmaninoff was born on one of his grandparents' estates in Oneg, a region of Novgorod in the northwestern part of Russia. [1] Sergei's parents were wealthy landowners and provided him with a comfortable childhood for the first ten years of his life. His father's poor handling of the family affairs generated a crisis that ended not only in the parents' divorce, but also in a radical change in life style with Sergei and his mother moving to a small flat in Saint Petersburg.

Sergei displayed natural talent for the piano at an early age and his mother arranged for a graduate student from the Saint Petersburg Conservatory to teach him in their home. Rachmaninoff did not do well and, upon the suggestion of his cousin Alexander Siloti, moved to Moscow in 1886, joining the piano studio of Nikolai Zverev. Siloti was already a renowned pianist, having just returned from several years in Weimar, where he studied under Franz Liszt.

Photo credit: George Grantham Bain collection @ wikipedia.com

Nikolai Zverev was a famous pedagogue in Moscow, teaching privately and at the junior division of the Moscow Conservatory. He also kept up to three talented piano students as boarders tuition free. Rachmaninoff joined Matvei Pressman and Leonid Maximov in this capacity. In this new environment, Rachmaninoff spent hours practicing piano and studied other musical subjects.

In 1888, at age 16, Sergei was admitted in the conservatory's senior department as a student of Siloti. Three years later, disagreements between Vladimir Safonov, the powerful new director of the Conservatory, and Alexander Siloti resulted in Siloti's resignation from his post at the Moscow Conservatory. Not interested in changing piano teachers for his last year of study, Rachmaninoff was allowed to finish his studies one year earlier than normal.

Many successful compositions appeared during the early 1890s, including the Prelude in C-sharp minor. In 1897, however, bad reviews of his first symphony drove Rachmaninoff to the edge of depression. For a few years he could not find inspiration to compose and started a conducting career. After consultations with Dr. Nikolai Dahl in psychotherapy sessions that may have involved hypnotic suggestion, Sergei returned to composition with full force and immediately composed several works that became worldwide successes. The list includes the famous Piano Concerto in C minor, one of the most-often performed and recorded concertos in the piano repertoire.

In 1902, Rachmaninoff married his cousin Natalya Satina, and in 1903 their first daughter, Irina, was born. The family was complete in 1907 with the birth of their youngest daughter Tatiana.

The events that culminated in the 1917 revolution in Russia forced Rachmaninoff to emigrate with his young family. Needing to find ways to support his family outside his homeland, Rachmaninoff turned to piano performance as his main source of income. From that period until his death in 1943 he was a constant presence as a celebrated soloist with the best orchestras and in the most important concert venues in Europe and the United States.

Most of his piano works were composed before he left Russia. His only concerto composed after 1917 (No. 4 in G minor, Op. 40) was never received with the same enthusiasm as the previous two concertos (C minor and D minor), and the other two major piano works (*Variations on a Theme by Corelli*, Op. 42 and *Rhapsody on a Theme of Paganini*, Op. 43) are variations on foreign themes. It is almost as if Russia and piano music were so interconnected in his nature that away from his homeland Rachmaninoff could not find the inspiration to compose piano masterworks on his own themes. He never returned to his beloved Russia.

PERFORMANCE NOTES

Rachmaninoff's Piano Music

Fingering

When available, Rachmaninoff's own fingerings are shown in italics. Fingerings that are editorial have in mind a medium-sized hand. Some adjustments may be needed for smaller hands. As a rule, fingerings were carefully chosen to convey the phrasing and articulation, not simply for comfort. Two numbers connected by a hyphen represent a slide between black and white keys; two numbers connected by a slur represent finger substitution. In some cases, an optional fingering is shown under or above in parenthesis. Distribution of notes among hands is mostly original. Exceptions are noted in the score.

Pedaling

It is extremely difficult to notate pedaling in an effective way, especially when dealing with such complex pianistic textures as Rachmaninoff's. Good pedaling depends on many variables (quality of the instrument, performer's touch, how far the pedal is pressed, specific acoustics, etc.), and any effort becomes almost pointless, since the performer will need to make the final decisions using his or her musical abilities and sensibilities. Therefore, pedal indications are omitted with the exception of Rachmaninoff's own pedal marking in a few places. It is assumed that performers working on these pieces will have the necessary skills for a successful choice of pedaling. Use the pedal in such a way so the textures are always clear and not compromised by excessive blurring. Listen to the accompanying recording for ideas on possible pedaling.

Metronome Markings

Metronome markings are editorial suggestions. Rachmaninoff typically did not provide metronome markings for his works. When available his markings are meant only as basic indications of tempo; the music requires a refined flexibility and an organic rubato.

Dynamics and Articulation

Dynamics and articulations are Rachmaninoff's. Considered a very thorough proof-reader, Rachmaninoff was very consistent in his writing. There were virtually no inconsistencies in the articulation and phrase markings in the first editions, editions based on autographs, and modern editions. See the notes below on the individual pieces for a discussion on the minor discrepancies between editions.

Rachmaninoff's Preludes

The collection of 24 piano preludes, one in every major and minor key, was not composed at once. The earliest prelude is the one that has became almost synonymous with Rachmaninoff's name: the celebrated Prelude in C-sharp minor, Op. 3, No. 2, composed in 1892 and dedicated to his composition teacher, Anton Arensky. Later came ten preludes published as opus 23, composed from 1901–1903. This set is dedicated to his cousin, celebrated pianist Alexander Siloti. Siloti was instrumental not only in Rachmaninoff's piano instruction (first by placing him under Zverev and then as teacher at the Moscow Conservatory) but also in his private life, providing generous financial support to the struggling young composer. Siloti was the first pianist to perform the complete set of the opus 23 preludes in 1904. [2]

In 1910, fresh after his successful tour and premiere of his third piano concerto in the United States, Rachmaninoff completed the final thirteen preludes, published as opus 32. It is assumed that Rachmaninoff came up with the idea of composing a cycle of 24 preludes in all keys mirroring Chopin's set of Preludes, Op. 28, the classic example of this genre, and Scriabin's opus 11 which were very well-received by critics and audiences. It was only natural for Rachmaninoff to contribute to this tradition. The thirteen preludes of opus 32 covered all remaining keys left out of the previous, and returned to the same tonic (D-flat/C-sharp) of the first prelude, ending the set with a broad cyclical arch.

Preludes, Op. 32

In a letter to Morozov written on July 31, 1910 mentioning his summer work, Rachmaninoff comments: ". . . worst of all goes the business of the little piano pieces . . ." [3] These preludes were written in the keys necessary to complete a cycle of twenty four preludes which included the ten preludes from opus 23 and the Prelude in C-sharp minor, Op. 3, No. 2. During the same period, Rachmaninoff composed a sacred choral work, the *Liturgy of St John Chrysostom*, Op. 31 and a group of etudes, published in 1911 as *Etudes-Tableaux*, Op. 33.

The years between the composition of preludes from opus 23 and opus 32 were years of travel for Rachmaninoff. After spending some time in Italy, Germany and a grueling tour in the United States, Rachmaninoff and his family settled on the Ivanovka estate.

Considering the pianistic style of both sets of preludes, one could make a broad comparison, relating opus 23 to the second piano concerto and opus 32 to the third piano concerto. The texture in the preludes opus 32 tends to be more complex, polyphonic, and display motivic phrasing, a characteristic already shown in the first set, but taken here to new proportions.

It is interesting to observe a couple of textural elements that permeate this set, making it more unified than opus 23. One of the most important is the rhythmic figure

which is found in almost every measure of the Preludes in B-flat minor and B Major. The motive also has an important role in the Prelude in B minor (mm. 1–19 and the return of the same theme after the cadenza in m. 49). This rhythmic figure also appears briefly in the Prelude in D-flat Major (mm. 11–17), and in a less obvious way, augmented in the initial octaves of the Prelude in E minor. Another interesting feature is Rachmaninoff's use of repeated, large chords, combined with strong bass notes to create culminating moments. Clear examples of these can be found in the Prelude in B minor (mm. 18–36) and the Prelude in D-flat Major (mm. 40–41).

Notes on the Individual Pieces

Prelude in C Major, Op. 32, No. 1

Only 41 measures long and under 2 minutes of performance time, this is one of the shortest preludes in this set. It brings to mind Chopin's short Prelude in C Major, Op. 28, No. 1 as well as Liszt's first transcendental etude. A hint of the descending main motive (A–G-sharp–C-sharp) from Rachmaninoff's famous Prelude in C-sharp minor, Op. 3, No. 2 is present here, transposed to C minor:

Apart from the relationship to the Prelude in C-sharp minor, Op. 3, No. 2, there is also a relationship to the last prelude in D-flat Major. It gives a nice sense of proportion and even a cyclical feeling to the set of 24 preludes. As usual, in Rachmaninoff's piano music, the technical difficulties are pianistic, and it takes just an initial play-through to feel that sense of comfort. In contrast to opus 23, where original fingerings were kept to a minimum, in opus 32 Rachmaninoff wrote very detailed fingering. Quite often, however, the original fingering becomes very difficult or impossible for someone with small hands. Rachmaninoff's hands were not only very large, but he also had an incredible span between his fingers. Rachmaninoff's suggested fingering for the right hand in measure 22 is a good example: a diminished seventh played with fingers 3 and 5. Pay attention to the composer's articulation indications in the beginning (mm. 1–4 and similar), using the wrist to perform the short, repeated thirds.

Prelude in B-flat minor, Op. 32, No. 2

After spending several months working in the composition of a sacred work (*Liturgy of St John Chrysostom*, Op. 31), it is only natural that some religious character transpires in other pieces. This is the case with the Prelude in B-flat minor. The ostinato rhythm that permeates this reflective prelude (present in each measure with the exception of mm. 32–35) will be used again in the Preludes in B minor and D-flat Major. The section beginning in m. 17 starts a wave-like *crescendo* (from **pp**–**mf**, then from **p**–**ff**) and *accelerando*, culminating in a dramatic, two-measure **ff** (mm. 25–26). Throughout the prelude, lean a little on the first note of the dotted-rhythm motive, playing all three notes under one gesture. In the *allegro* section, use wrist rotation and pivoting fingers.

Prelude in E Major, Op. 32, No. 3

The religious character continues with this joyous prelude, bringing out one of Rachmaninoff's musical signatures: bells, bells and more bells! The performer of this prelude is challenged to display great dynamic contrasts, from *ff* to *pp*. A wise use of pedal will help create the necessary ringing sound. Flexible wrists will keep the loud chords moving and horizontal. Don't fall for a typical mistake in this prelude: playing it too loud and too vertical. Bells ring and move. Make your chords do the same. Rachmaninoff's fingering for the left hand in measure 6 and similar places once again reflects the large span of his hand. Playing the last beat of this measure with the implied 1-2-4-5 fingering (resulting in a sixth between G-sharp and B to be reached by fingers 2 and 4), especially at a fast speed, is very uncomfortable for a normally-sized hand. The suggested fingering (1-2-5-4) allows for a better rotation and more hand stability.

Prelude in E minor, Op. 32, No. 4

One of the longest (158 measures, including the alternate *ossia* ending) and certainly the most difficult in this set, this prelude shows Rachmaninoff in his best symphonic style. The texture is layered, with distinctive, orchestral sonorities. Use your imagination and create your own orchestration (after listening to Rachmaninoff's orchestral music first) for this magnificent and powerful piece. The mood varies from majestic (trumpet beginning) to *scherzando* (section beginning in m. 27), to lyrical (*Lento* section, beginning in m. 53, which includes the measures with the thickest texture, mm. 62–70), culminating in a triumphant, *presto possible* section, with full chords played *fortissimo*. Only play this one if you feel really at ease with octaves and fast chordal textures. I suggest using the longer version (*ossia*) to end the prelude, where a quote from the oft-quoted *Dies irae* gives an extra religious touch to this powerful piece.

Prelude in G Major, Op. 32, No. 5

A bird song by a stream would be a suitable description of this charming prelude. The irregular rhythm—quintuplets in the left hand accompanying triplets in the right hand—resembles the freedom of nature, where nothing

is standard, but everything is proportional. Here the pianist is required to have complete rhythmic control, keeping the pulse steady with a slight *rubato* and allowing both hands to live "parallel lives." In the left hand, use some arm weight for the quarter notes while playing the remaining four notes of the quintuplets gently using only fingers; use a more intense arm weight to project the melody even at the *pp* level. The thirty-second note *leggiero* little turns should be played with the tips of the fingers and a fast but soft attack, creating a bright, while still soft sonority.

Prelude in F minor, Op. 32, No. 6

Another short *tour de force*, and to a certain extent similar to the initial Prelude in C Major. This prelude/etude is based on concise motives and never develops memorable melodic content. The piece requires dexterity and comfortable knowledge of the keyboard topography due to its use of the entire range of the instrument. In order to keep an appropriate balance between the layers, make sure that the sixteenth notes are light so the longer notes, especially the dotted quarter notes, can be expressive. Rachmaninoff was a very careful proof-reader of his scores, and printing mistakes are rare, especially when one considers the textural complexity of his music. One minor exception may be present in this prelude (see also notes for the Prelude in A minor); the section from m. 53 to 57 at the end of this prelude is marked by a powerful descending line in the left hand, a series of minor thirds:

In all editions reviewed, the third eight note in the left hand of measure 55 is A-flat, breaking the sequence. The correct note for the sequence to work would be F. A-flat also removes one of the characteristics of the F-minor triad in that passage, adding the third of the triad, where the other similar moments employ an empty triad without its third. The editor believes this to be an error not noticed by Rachmaninoff and perpetuated in all subsequent editions. Rachmaninoff's performance of this prelude "corrects" the error.

Prelude in F Major, Op. 32, No. 7

This prelude has a generally peaceful mood, but hints of uneasiness abound: intriguing harmonies, off-beat accompaniment chords, syncopations—all these elements help contribute to the ambiguous atmosphere of this interesting piece, which is unfortunately not performed as often as it should. Not technically demanding, it still poses some challenges, mainly related to voicing control, skips and the need for extended reach in certain chords. Once again, Rachmaninoff composed this piece with his hand size in mind. This edition suggests a different hand distribution that helps to bring out the polyphonic texture of this piece for pianists with a medium-sized hand. Rachmaninoff's inspiring recording of this prelude shows him in full control of *rubato*, with a clear definition of layers.

Prelude in A minor, Op. 32, No. 8

Similar to the Prelude in F minor, this piece is short, powerful, and in the style of an etude. It requires dexterity and great cross-hands technique. In this prelude, the editor believes that a minor error has been perpetuated through editions. This concerns m. 35 where right hand has a pattern of minor thirds followed by an octave. Most editions (with the exception of Dover and Masters Music, both reprints of early Russian editions) print a tenth (A–C) as the last right-hand sixteenth note:

The logical continuation would be an octave C-C, keeping the pattern and not adding a large interval in the middle of a very fast passage. There is not a recording of Rachmaninoff available for this prelude, and the passage is so fast that one can not clearly identify which notes, A or C, pianists usually perform. The editor suggests playing an octave. If you decide to keep with the original notation but are not able to reach a tenth at fast tempo, one solution would be to play the A with left hand. Notice that in the last measure, *f* applies only to the second beat; the first beat is still *pp*.

Prelude in A Major, Op. 32, No. 9

This prelude has the typical "Rachmaninoff warmth," with lush sonorities and a rich texture. The undulating octave line in the low register supports the rhythmic *ostinato* in the middle (one could call it the piece's "heartbeat"), both preparing the stage for the beautiful melody, marked **mf**. This melodic line, in its simplicity and depth, is formed by a downward leap of a sixth followed by a scale moving up. The editor suggests performing the *ossia* (mm. 15–17 and 19–20); they add a little difficulty to that section, but the effort is worthwhile. The ascending quadruplets add to the rhythmic drive, and the arrivals (second beats of mm. 17 and 21) become more pronounced and exciting. After a brief return of the main idea in the minor mode (mm. 29–30) and its quick tonal transitions through A-flat Major and F-sharp minor, we arrive at a fast, virtuosic passage (*Più vivo*) that obsessively repeats the falling initial sixths. Use wrist rotation in the right hand to avoid performing mm. 41–49 with fingers only.

Prelude in B minor, Op. 32, No. 10

Together with the Prelude in E minor and the Prelude in D-flat Major, this is one of the longest in the set. It is a well-known fact that Rachmaninoff drew inspiration from a painting by Swiss symbolist painter Arnold Böcklin titled *Die Heimkehr* (*The Return* or *The Homecoming*), reproduced on the front cover of this edition. This is the second time Rachmaninoff used a Böcklin painting as inspiration. He had previously based his symphonic work *Isle of the Dead*, Op. 29 on a Böcklin painting. The static character of this somber prelude brings to mind Liszt's "Il Penseroso," a piano work that also has extra-musical inspiration (based on a sculpture by Michelangelo). Unlike Liszt's work, this prelude is extended and includes a big culminating, chordal section (mm. 22–36), as well as a virtuosic passage (mm. 47–48) before returning to the starting mood. The main challenges in this prelude are textural; a successful performance of this piece will require full control of dynamics and a deep tonal control. From the very beginning, differentiate the dotted-rhythm motif from the accompanying chords. In the culminating section (mm. 22–36), play the melody with your whole upper torso while vibrating the repeated chords, keeping your hands close to the keys. This will create a full sound with a variety of colors, avoiding falling in the typical trap of being too loud for too long. Don't forget Rachmaninoff's "*tochka*": define the culminating point clearly for a successful and satisfying performance.

Prelude in B Major, Op. 32, No. 11

This peaceful and almost religious work is unusual in its textural simplicity, when compared to most other preludes by Rachmaninoff. It is chordal from the beginning to the end, not using any of the typical pianistic richness one expects from Rachmaninoff. It brings to mind the Prelude in D minor, Op. 23, No. 3. Several of the same skills are needed for a successful performance: good rhythmic and voicing control, plus the ability to play "horizontally" in a "vertical" texture. In order to enhance the richness of sound, pay special attention to the lowest and highest notes in each chord, creating a frame for it. Another challenge in this piece is the phrasing, which requires complete independence between the hands; in the right hand, slurs in some instances cover two measures (mm. 3–4, 7–8), while sometimes only one measure (mm. 9, 10, 11, 12), or connect partial measures (mm. 23–24, 24–25). Quite often, the left hand has slurs that don't match those of right hand, creating a very interesting, polyphonic phrasing.

Prelude in G-sharp minor, Op. 32, No. 12

One of the most often performed preludes in opus 32, this work is a masterpiece of conciseness. In only 48 measures and just over 2 minutes of performance time, Rachmaninoff is able to portray the beauty and vastness of his homeland. It could be interpreted as a description of winter: the coldness of the open fifth initial *arpeggio*, its fast motion and *crescendo* feeling like freezing wind; this contrasts with the warm melody played by left hand symbolizing someone confronting the elements, bringing human warmth to a cold landscape. Rachmaninoff's detailed tempo indications, almost in each measure, should be carefully followed, creating an organic *rubato*. Texturally, this prelude shows Rachmaninoff's wonderful control of the keyboard. The entire piece falls naturally under the fingers: the *ostinato* sixteenth notes are almost always played within one octave, while the left-hand melody is built mainly of small intervals. In measure 18 (fourth beat of the left hand), most editions omit a natural sign before the B. The harmonic motion of the previous two measures suggests that the chords in the fourth beats are followed by 4 sixteenth notes in the same harmony (observe the fourth beats of mm. 16 and 17). In the editor's opinion, a natural sign is needed in m. 18 in order for the harmony to remain consistent. There is not a Rachmaninoff recording of this prelude; however, in most recordings surveyed, pianists perform B natural.

Prelude in D-flat Major, Op. 32, No. 13

The last prelude is one of the longest and certainly one of the hardest. It brings back some thematic and rhythmic ideas from previous preludes; the rhythm in mm. 11–17 reminds one of the Prelude in B-flat minor and the Prelude in B Major, while the repeated *ff* chords of mm. 40–41 are similar to the long culminating section in the Prelude in B minor (see mm. 18–36 of that prelude). The most important and remarkable "flashback" is the return of the famous three-note motive from the Prelude in C-sharp minor, Op. 3, No. 2. The quote starts to appear in m. 31 in the left hand. The intervallic relationship is still not the exact one and the rhythm is still dotted. Beginning in m. 37, however, it is repeated 4 times in the original form. The famous A–G-sharp–C-sharp motive (mm. 37–39) is shown in an augmented form in the bass (mm. 40–42), culminating with the recapitulation of the main theme.

This prelude, with all its textural richness and harmonic warmth, ends the group of 24 preludes in an almost cyclical way. The pianistic texture in the section from mm. 21–26, with its right-hand polyphonic conversation supported by a low and undulating bass line, will be used in later pieces such as the Etude-tableaux in E-flat minor, Op. 39, No. 5. The return of the main theme in m. 42 is very full, with a thick texture. Extended chords abound (see mm. 46–49), and are impossible to perform blocked, as written. This edition suggests a different hand distribution and even omitting certain notes in cases when they are duplicated in the chords. The rhythm in m. 60 should be felt in eight notes, and the extended chords can be performed with the fingering suggested.

Notes:

[1] There has been confusion about Rachmaninoff's real birthplace. He always mentioned Oneg as his birthplace, but some scholars believe he was born at Semyonovo, and moved to Oneg because of his father's unfortunate financial decisions.

[2] Several sources indicate February 10, 1903 as the first complete performance of op. 23. However, according to Apetian (Rachmaninoff: Letters, p. 222), only three preludes were performed by the composer on that day: prelude in F-sharp minor, B-flat Major and G minor. Siloti's performance of opus 23, according to Antipov, was on November 13, 1904, in St. Petersburg.

[3] Bertensson and Leyda, p. 168.

Editions Consulted:

Preludes, Op. 32

Rachmaninoff, Sergei. *Preludes for the Piano, Op. 32*. New York: G. Schirmer, Inc., 1942.

Rachmaninoff, Sergei. *Thirteen Preludes, Opus 32*. Edited by Ruth Laredo. New York: Edition Peters, 1990.

Complete Preludes, Op. 3, No. 2; Op. 23; and Op. 32

Rachmaninoff, Sergei. *Complete Preludes and Etudes-Tableaux*. New York: Dover Publications, Inc.,1988.

Rachmaninoff, Sergei. *Preludes Op. 3 No. 2, Op. 23 and Op. 32*. Van Nuys, California: Alfred Music Publishing, 1988.

Rachmaninoff, Sergei. *Preludes Op. 3 No. 2, Op. 23 and Op. 32*. Edited by Robert Threlfall. London: Boosey & Hawkes, 1992.

Rachmaninoff, Sergei. *Preludes Op. 3 No. 2, Op. 23 and Op. 32*. New York: G. Schirmer, Inc., 1994.

Rachmaninoff, Sergei. *Preludes Op. 3 No. 2, Op. 23 and Op. 32*. Moscow: Russian Music Publishing/ Bärenreiter, 2006.

Rachmaninoff, Sergei. *Twenty-four Preludes for Solo Piano, Op. 3 No. 2, Opp. 23, 32*. Edited by Pavel Lamm. Boca Raton, FL: Masters Music Publications, Inc., 1948.

Bibliography:

Apetian, Zarui, editor. *S.V. Rachmaninoff: Pis'ma*. Moscow: State Musical Publisher, 1955.

Bertensson, Sergei, and Jay Leyda. *Sergei Rachmaninoff: A Lifetime in Music*. New York: New York University Press, 1956.

Haylock, Julian. *Sergei Rachmaninov: An Essential Guide to His Life and Works*. London: Pavilion Books 1997.

Lui-Tawaststjerna, Hui-Ying. *Rachmaninoff's Prelude in C-sharp minor, Op. 3, No 2: The Composer's Notation and His Three Interpretations*. Helsinki: Sibelius Academy, 2004.

Norris, Geoffrey. *Rakhmaninov*. London: J. M. Dent & Sons Ltd, 1976.

Scott, Michael. *Rachmaninoff*. Stroud, Gloucestershire: The History Press Ltd., 2008.

Seroff, Victor I. *Rachmaninoff* . New York: Books for Libraries Press, 1950.

CD Credits:

Lance Miller, Recording Engineer

Alexandre Dossin, Producer and Pianist

Recorded at Beall Concert Hall, University of Oregon School of Music and Dance

Preludes, Op. 32
I

Sergei Rachmaninoff
Op. 32, No. 1

Allegro vivace [♩ = 80]

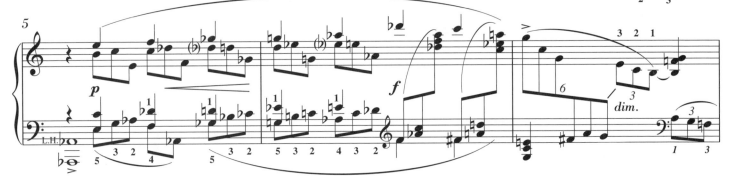

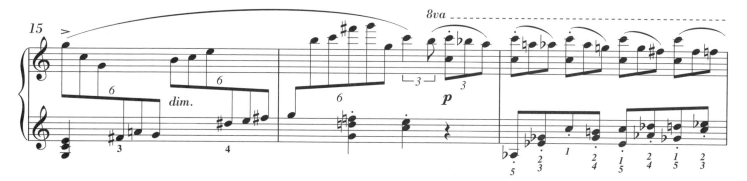

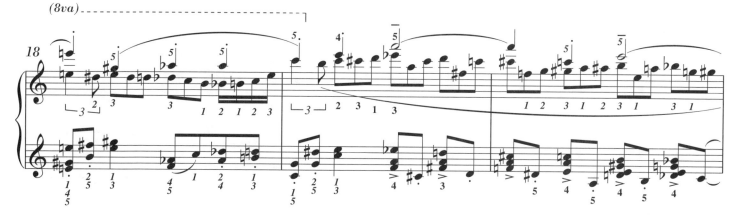

II

Sergei Rachmaninoff
Op. 32, No. 2

Allegretto [♩. = 60]

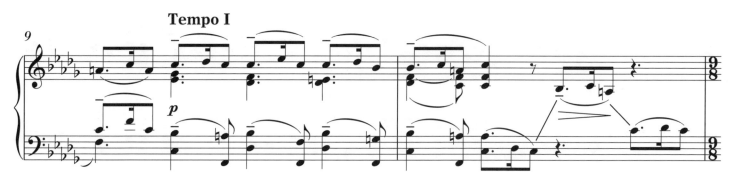

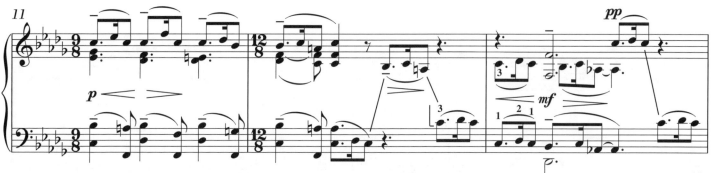

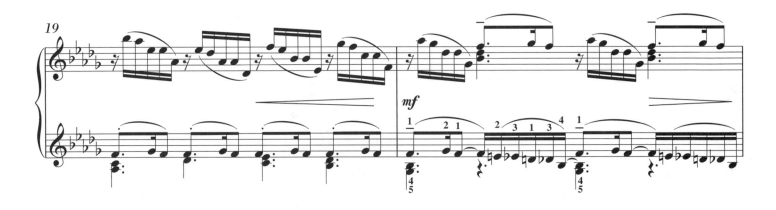

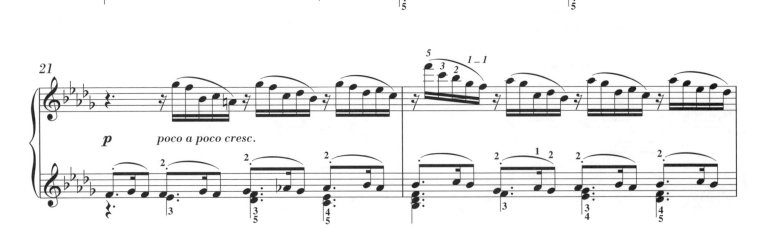

Allegro

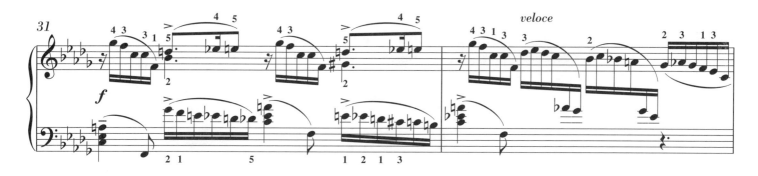

Meno mosso

Allegro moderato [♩· = 70]

Allegro scherzando [♩· = 74]

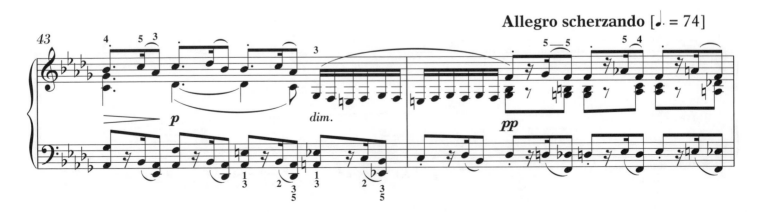

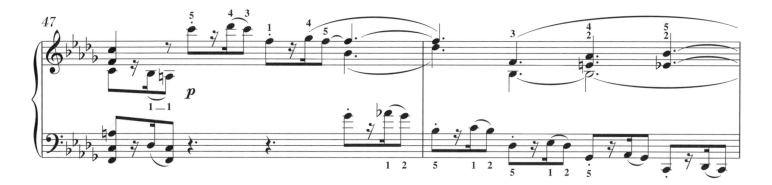

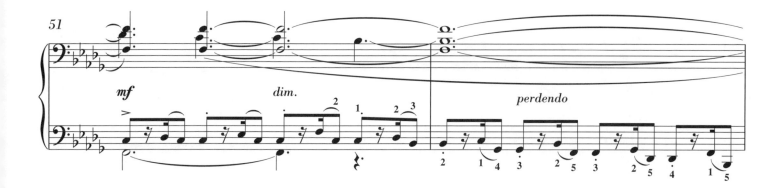

III

Sergei Rachmaninoff
Op. 32, No. 3

Allegro vivace [♩ = 120]

Meno mosso [♩ = 90] **Tempo I**

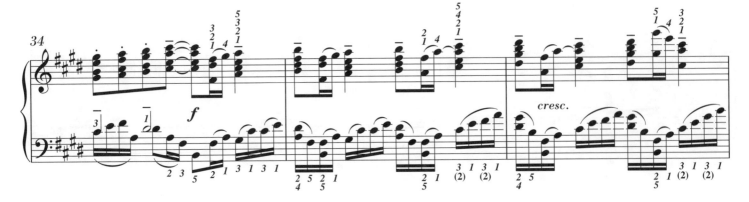

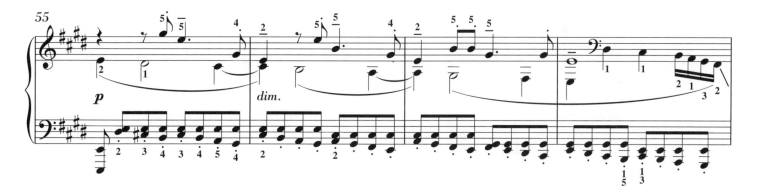

IV

Sergei Rachmaninoff
Op. 32, No. 4

Allegro con brio [♩ = 100]

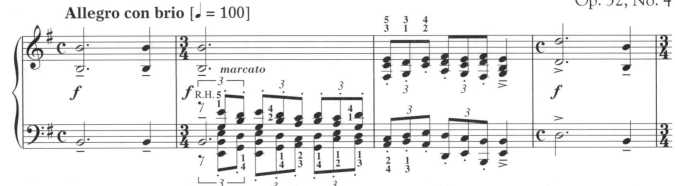

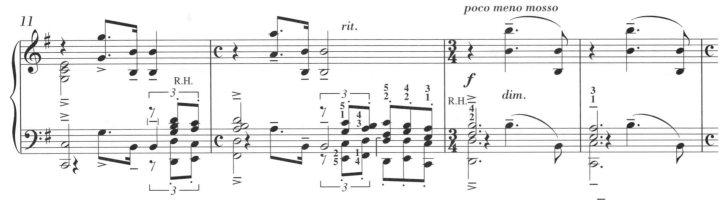

Poco meno mosso

Tempo I

Lento [♩. = 65]

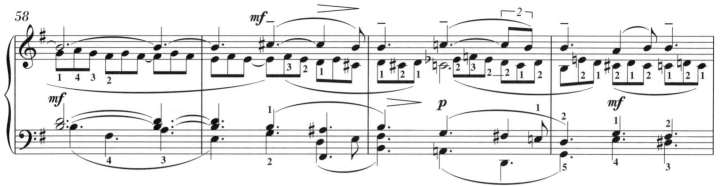

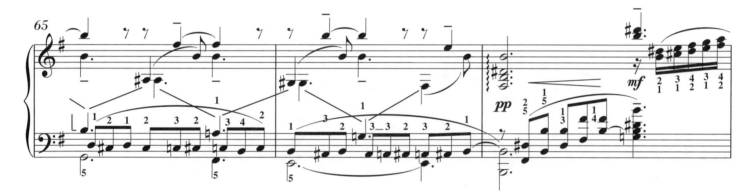

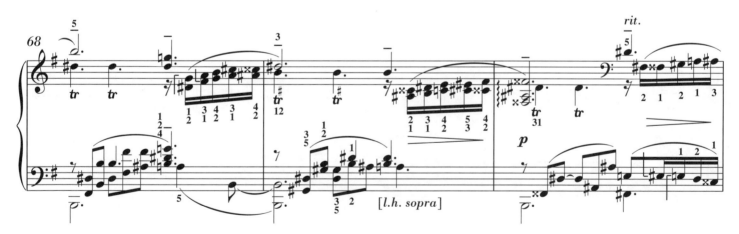

Tempo I

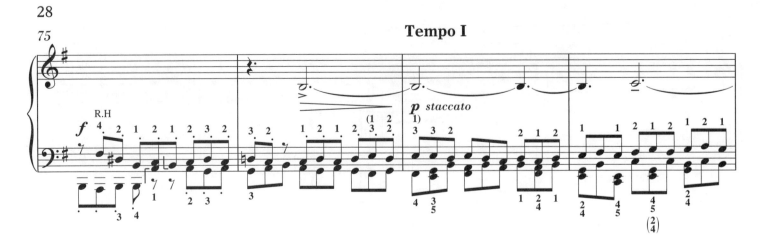

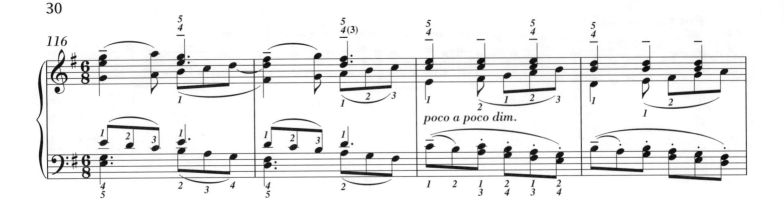

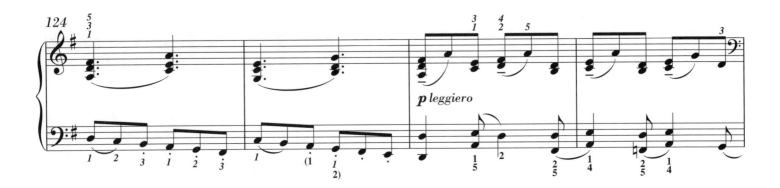

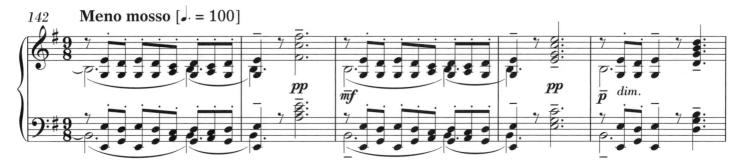

*Ossia:

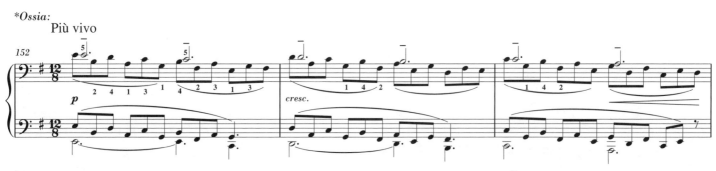

V

Sergei Rachmaninoff
Op. 32, No. 5

Moderato [♩ = 60]

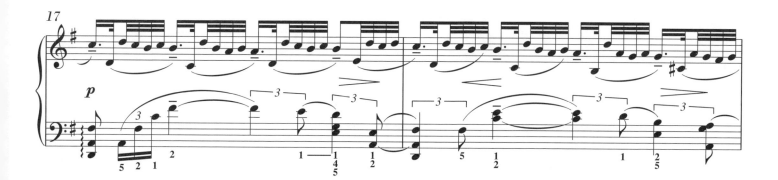

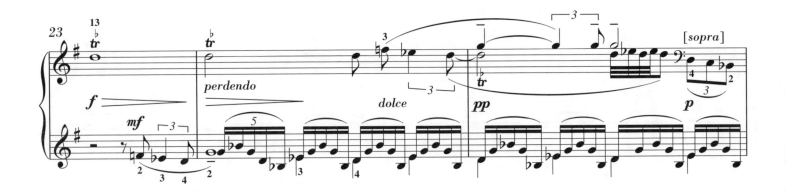

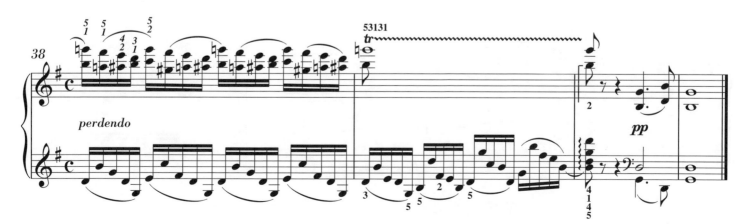

VI

Sergei Rachmaninoff
Op. 32, No. 6

Allegro appassionato [♩ = 100]

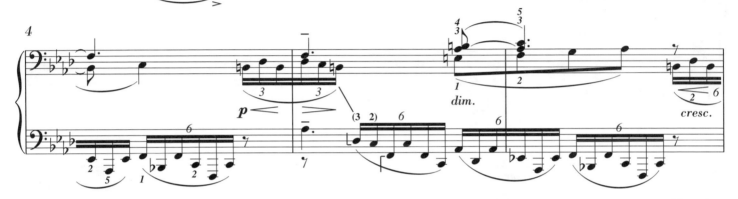

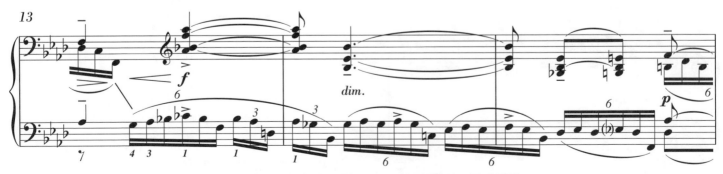

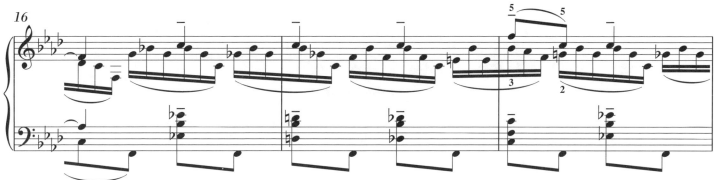

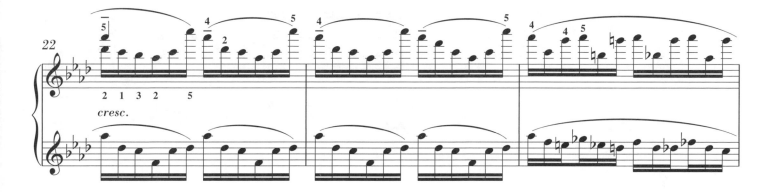

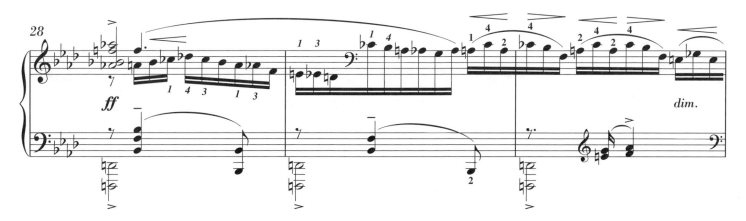

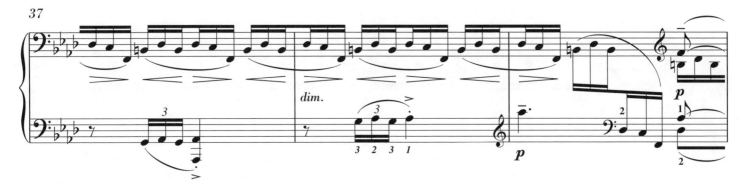

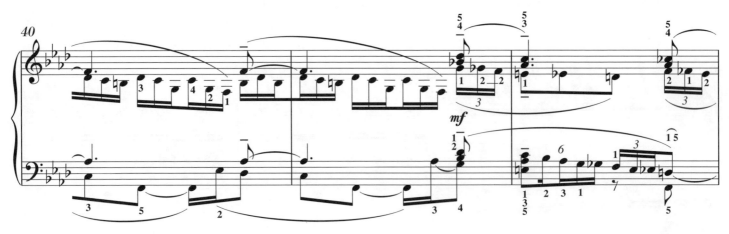

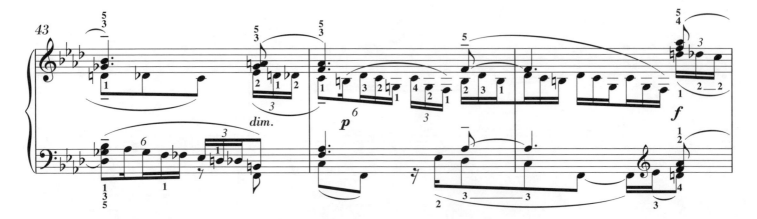

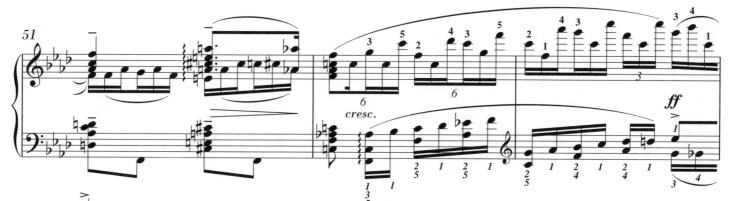

* See performance notes for this prelude (pg. 7).

VII

Sergei Rachmaninoff
Op. 32, No. 7

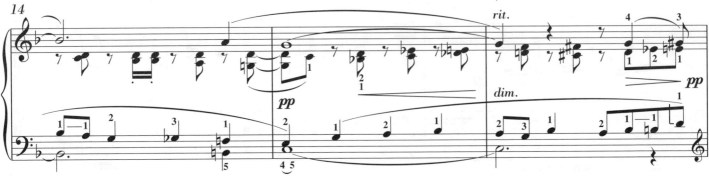

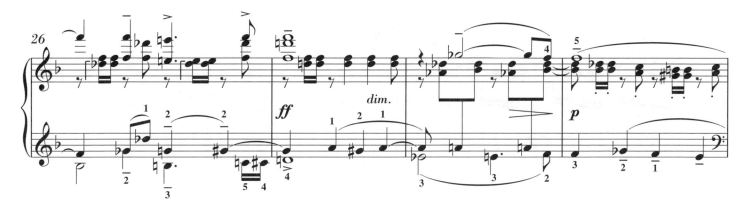

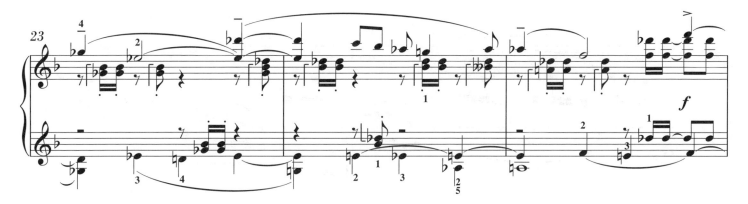

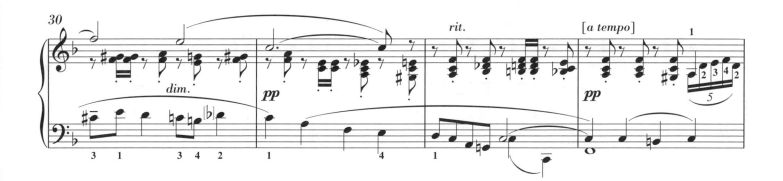

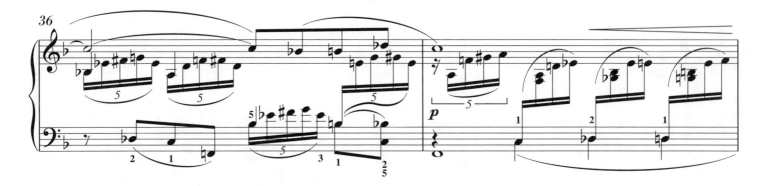

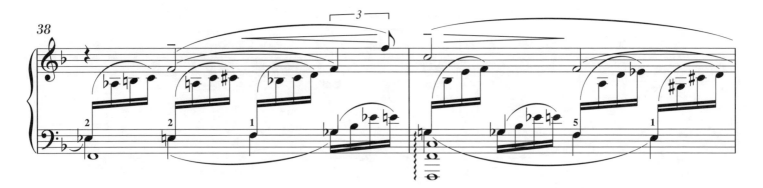

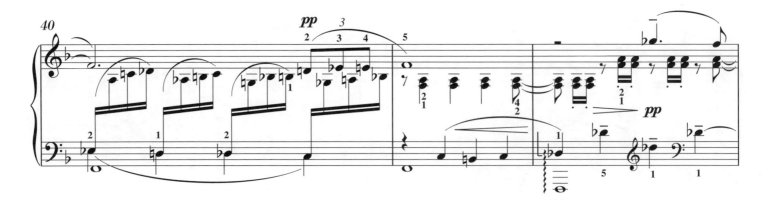

VIII

Sergei Rachmaninoff
Op. 32, No. 8

Vivo [♩ = 140]

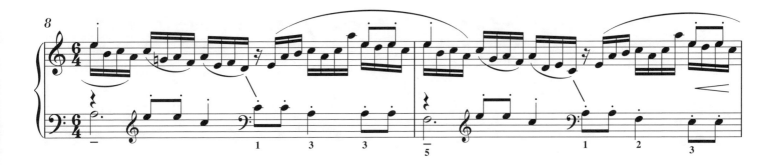

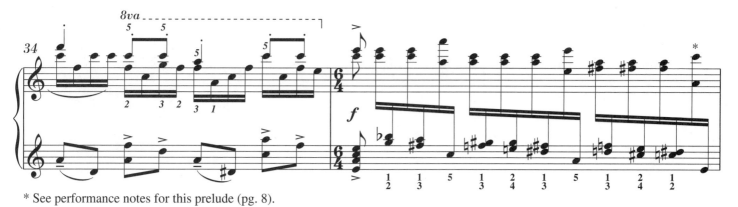

* See performance notes for this prelude (pg. 8).

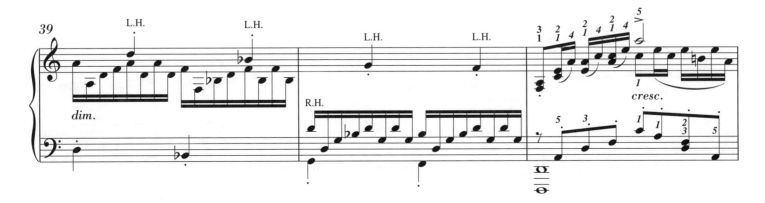

IX

Sergei Rachmaninoff
Op. 32, No. 9

Allegro moderato [♩. = 60]

* Play the lower two notes with the thumb; use the knuckle for the black key, and the nail for the white key. Also in similar places.

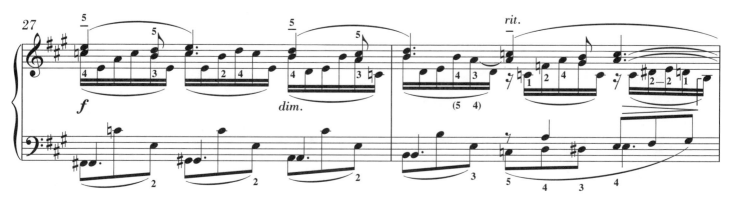

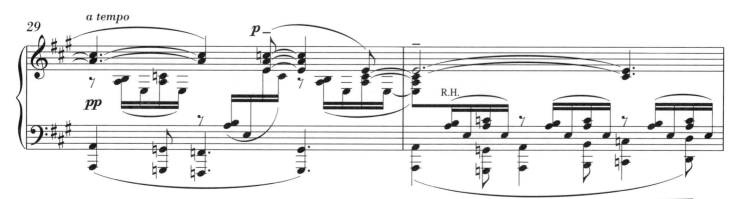

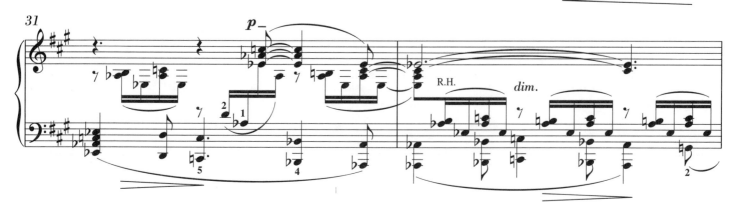

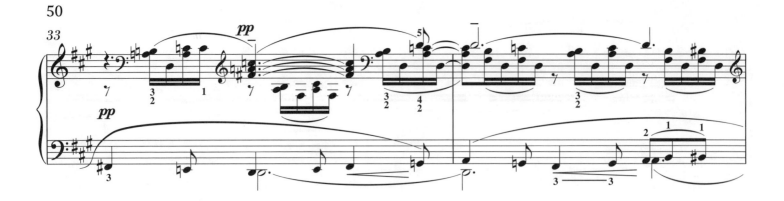

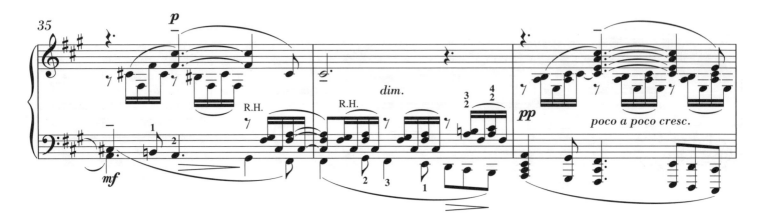

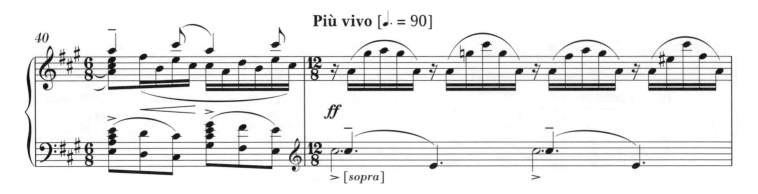

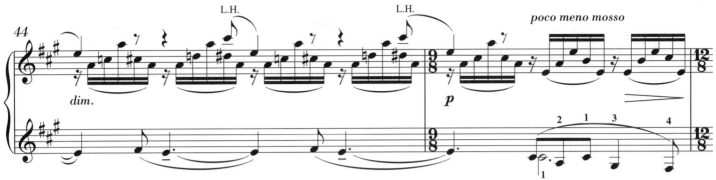

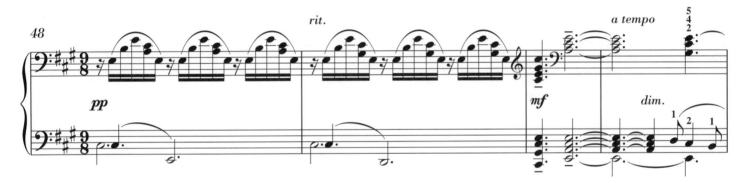

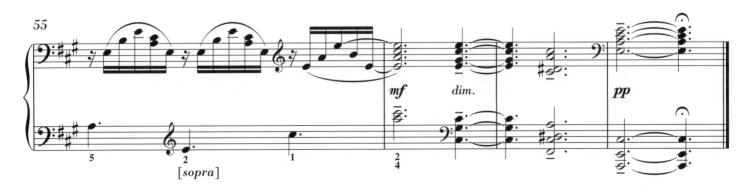

X

Sergei Rachmaninoff
Op. 32, No. 10

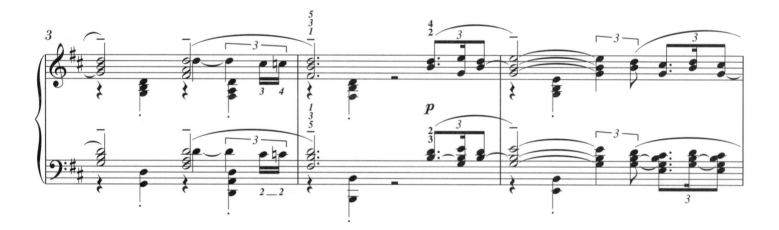

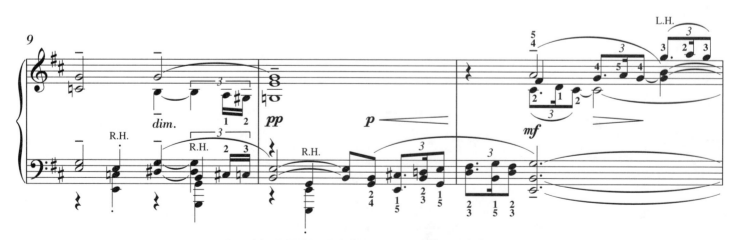

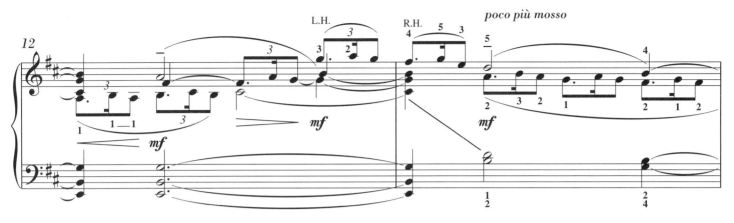

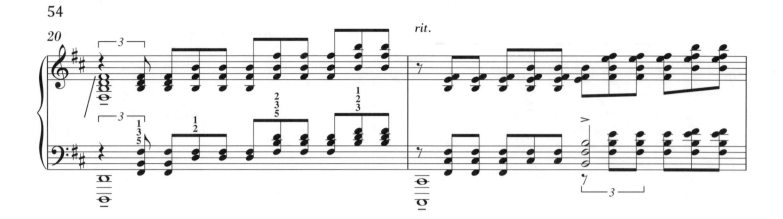

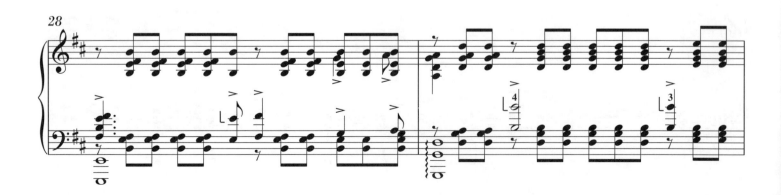

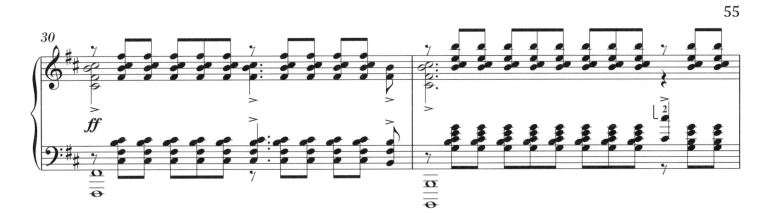

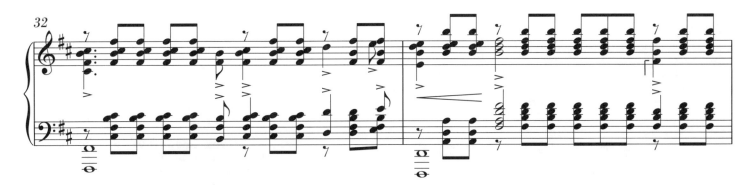

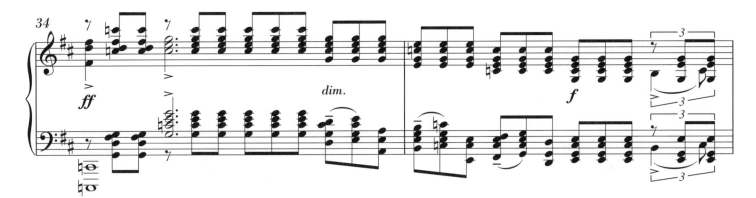

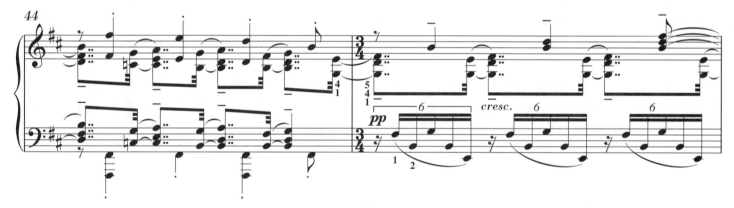

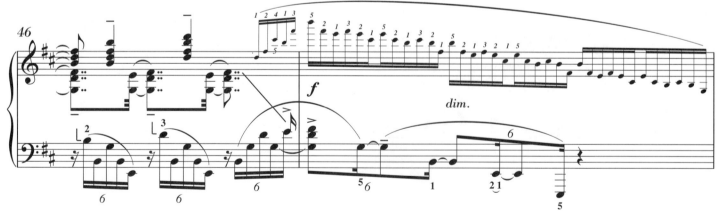

A tempo, come prima

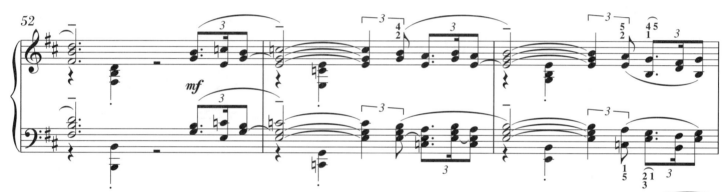

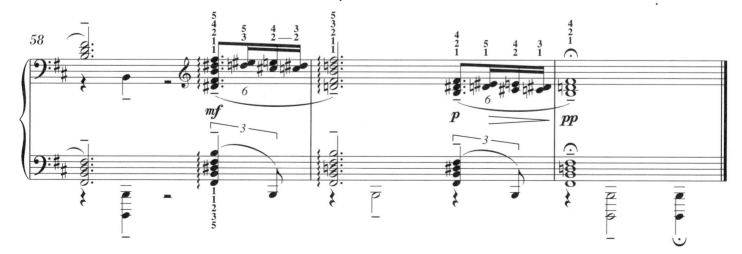

XI

Sergei Rachmaninoff
Op. 32, No. 11

Allegretto [♩. = 50]

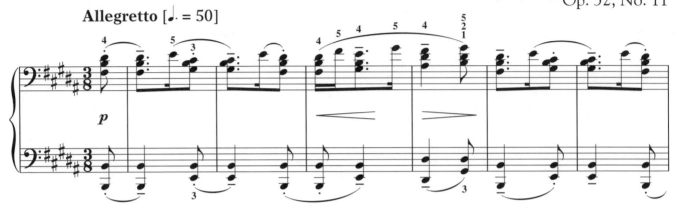

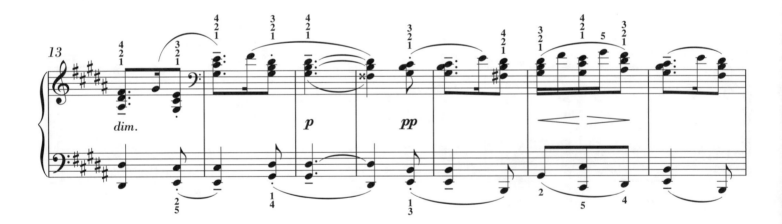

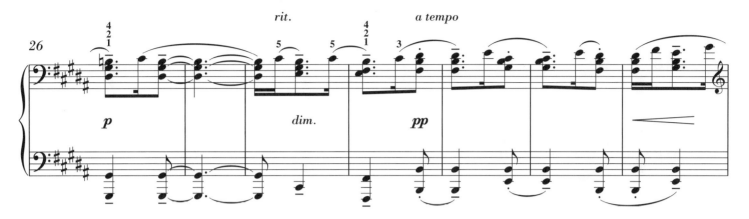

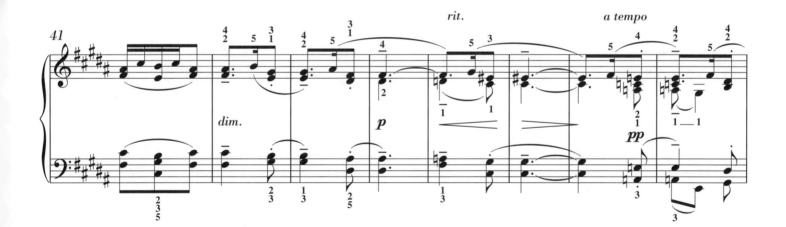

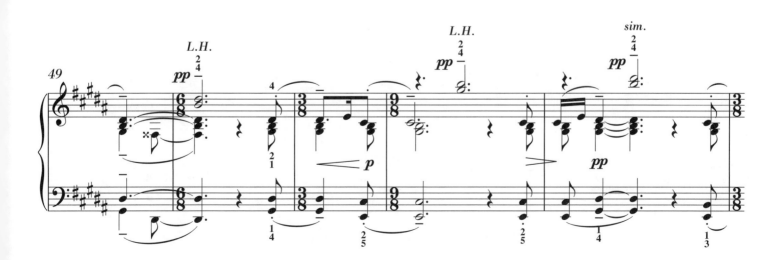

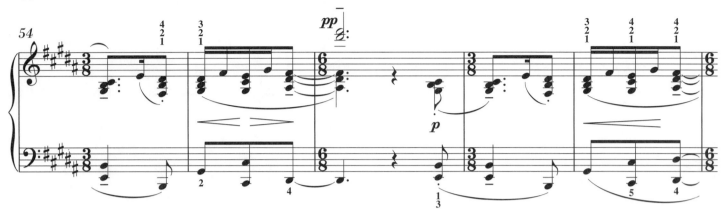

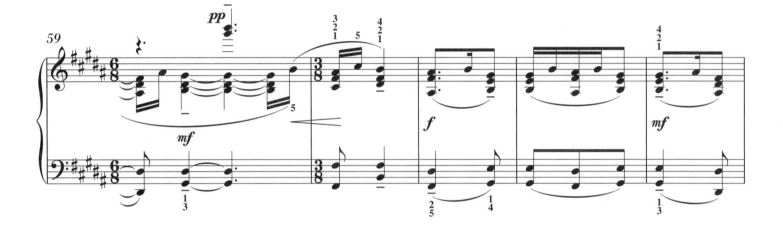

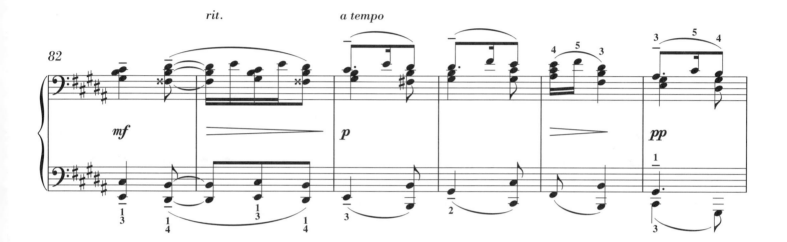

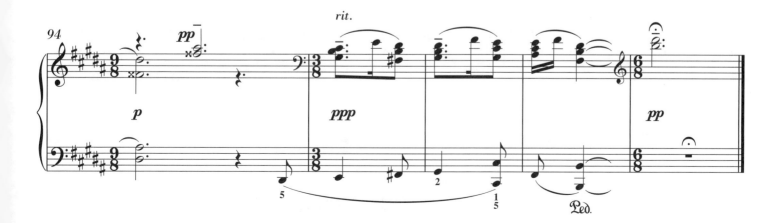

XII

Sergei Rachmaninoff
Op. 32, No. 12

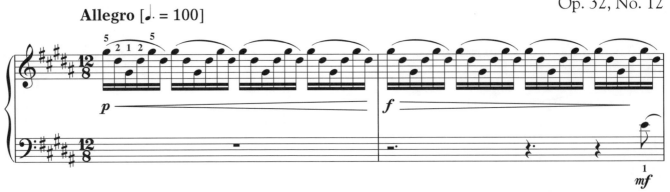

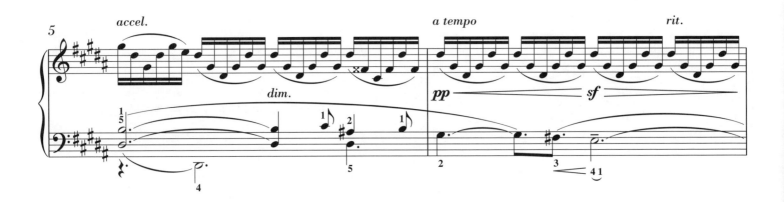

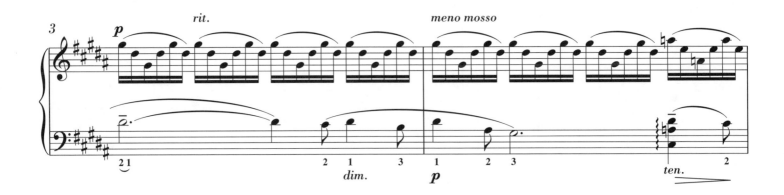

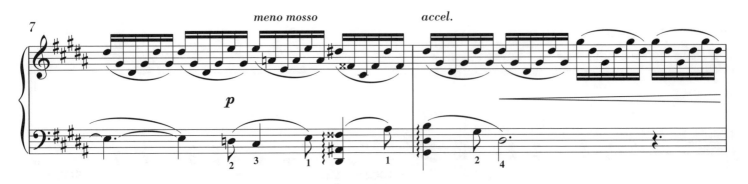

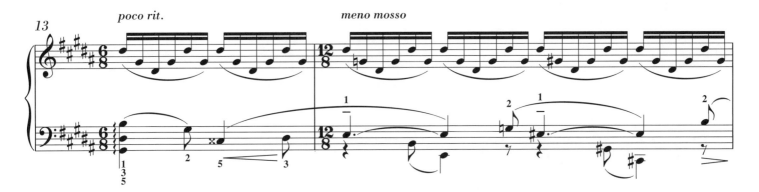

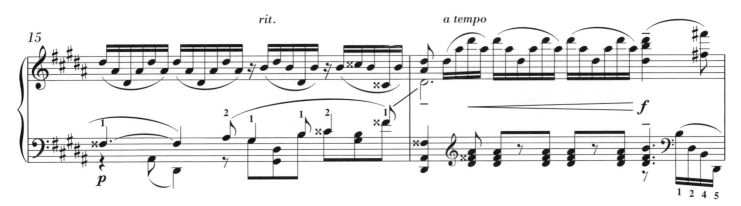

* See performance notes for this prelude (pg. 9).

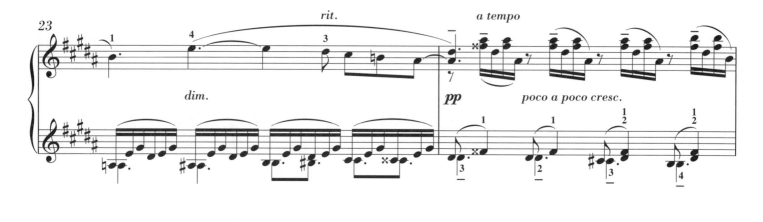

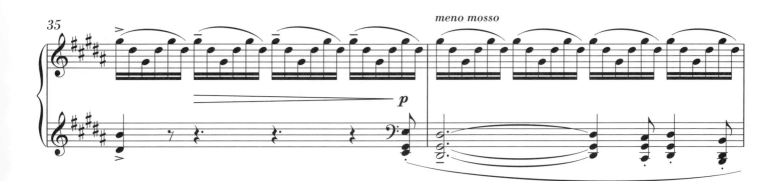

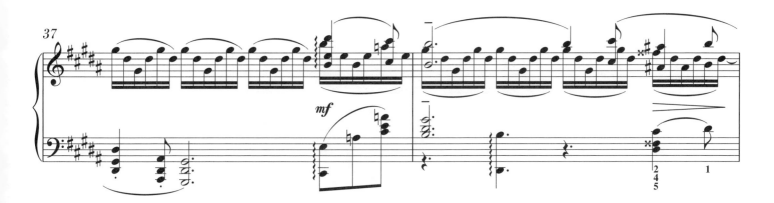

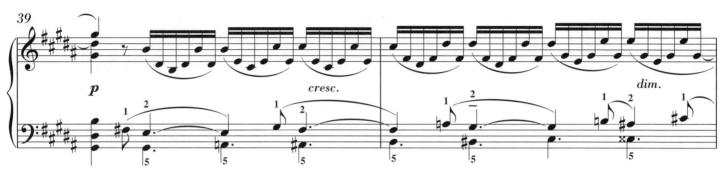

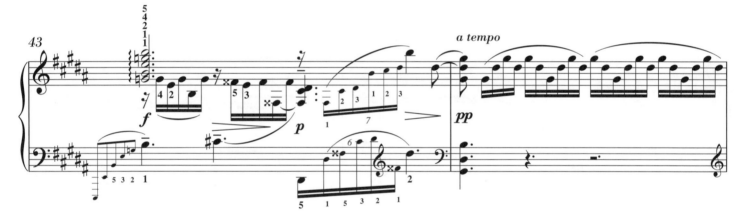

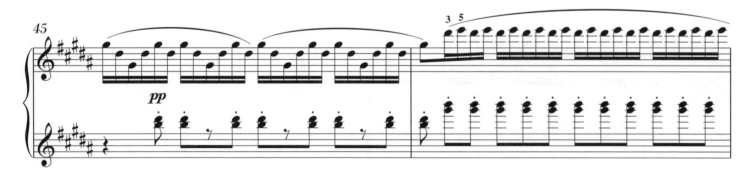

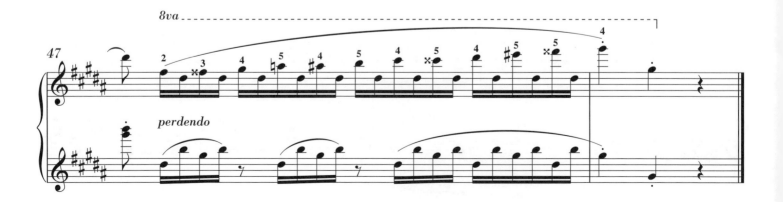

XIII

Sergei Rachmaninoff
Op. 32, No. 13

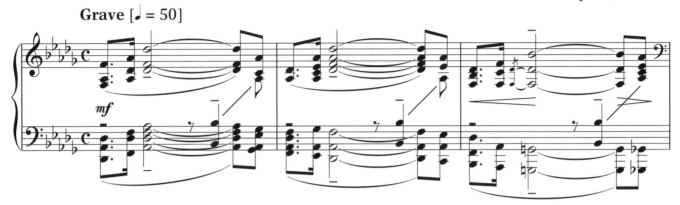

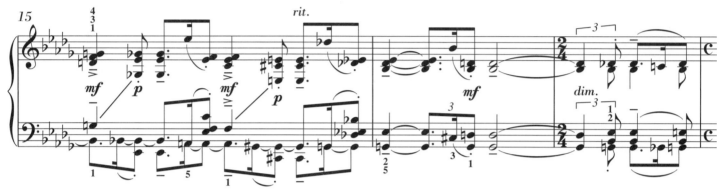

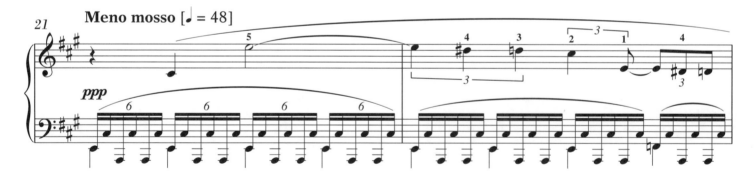

* Some editions print G-flat.

Allegro [♩ = 70]

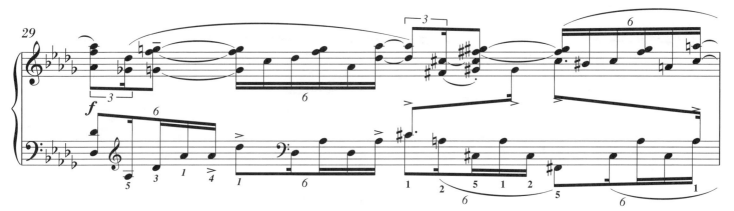

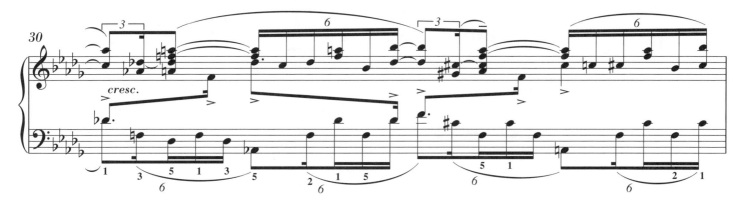

più vivo

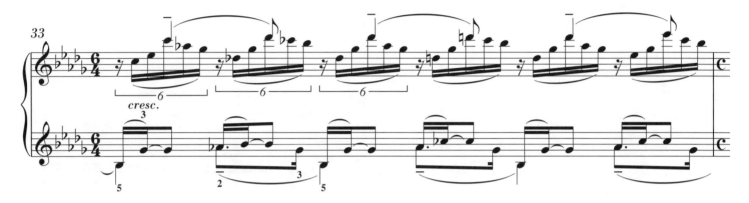

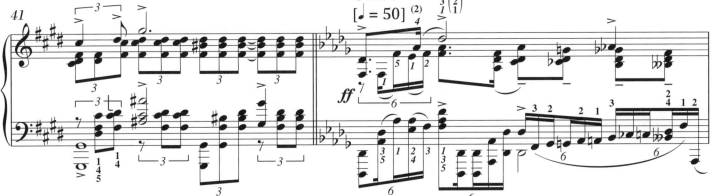

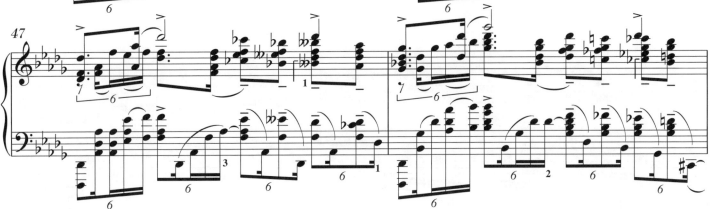

* The B-flat may be omitted.

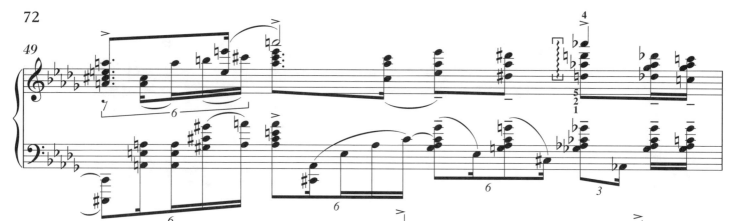

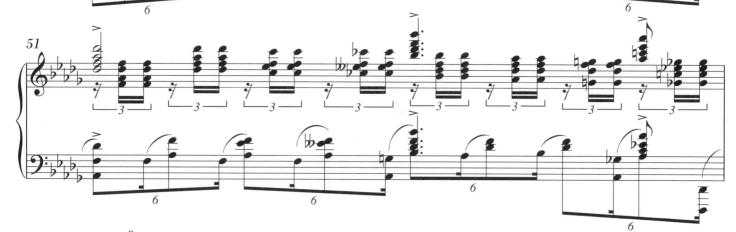

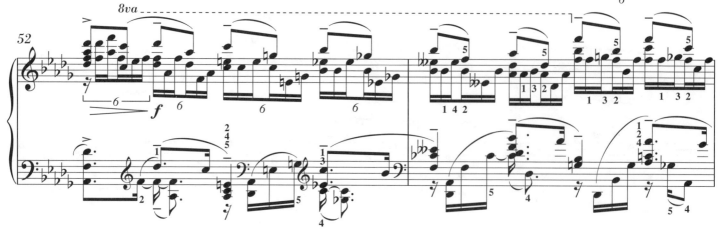

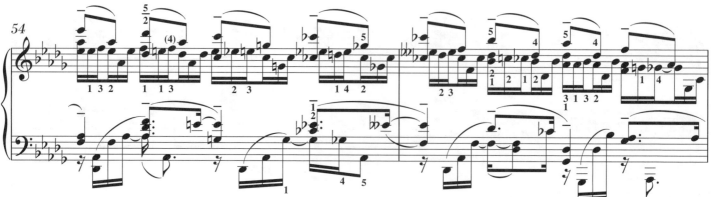

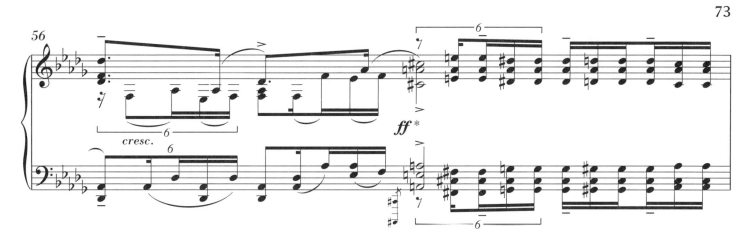

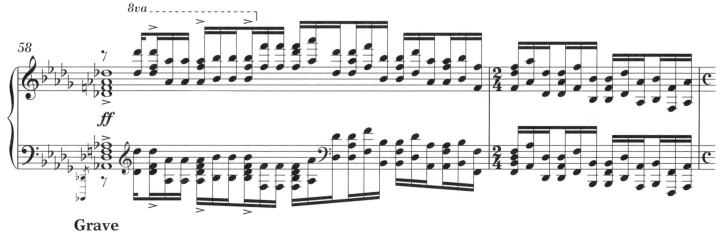

Grave

* Some editions print *f*.

ABOUT THE EDITOR

ALEXANDRE DOSSIN

Considered by Martha Argerich an "extraordinary musician" and by international critics a "phenomenon" and "a master of contrasts," Alexandre Dossin keeps active performing, recording, and teaching careers.

Born in Brazil, where he lived until he was nineteen, Dossin spent nine years studying in Moscow, Russia, before establishing residency in the United States. This background allows him to be fluent in several languages and equally comfortable in a wide range of piano repertoire.

Currently on the faculty of the University of Oregon School of Music, Dossin is a graduate from the University of Texas-Austin and the Moscow Tchaikovsky Conservatory in Russia. He studied with and was an assistant of Sergei Dorensky at the Tchaikovsky Conservatory, and William Race and Gregory Allen at UT-Austin.

A prizewinner in several international piano competitions, Dossin received the First Prize and the Special Prize at the 2003 Martha Argerich International Piano Competition in Buenos Aires, Argentina. Other awards include the Silver Medal and Second Honorable Mention in the Maria Callas Grand Prix and Third Prize and Special Prize in the Mozart International Piano Competition.

He performed numerous live recitals for public radio in Texas, Wisconsin, and Illinois, including returning engagements at the Dame Myra Hess Memorial Concert Series. Dossin has performed in over twenty countries, including international festivals in Japan, Canada, the United States, Brazil, and Argentina, on some occasions sharing the stage with Martha Argerich. He was a soloist with the Brazilian Symphony, Buenos Aires Philharmonic, Mozarteum Symphony, and São Paulo Symphony, having collaborated with renowned conductors such as Charles Dutoit, Michael Gielen, Isaac Karabtchevsky, Keith Clark, and Eleazar de Carvalho.

Dossin has CDs released by Musicians Showcase Recording (2002), Blue Griffin (*A Touch of Brazil*, 2005), and Naxos (*Verdi-Liszt Paraphrases*, 2007; *Kabalevsky Complete Sonatas and Sonatinas*, 2009; *Kabalevsky Complete Preludes*, 2009; *Liszt in Russia*, 2011), praised in reviews by *Diapason*, *The Financial Times*, *Fanfare Magazine*, *American Record Guide*, *Clavier* and other international publications.

In the United States, Alexandre Dossin was featured as the main interview and on the cover of *Clavier* magazine and interviewed by *International Piano Magazine* (South Korea). He is an editor and recording artist for several Schirmer Performance Editions.

Dossin is a member of the Board of Directors for the American Liszt Society and the President of the Oregon Chapter of the American Liszt Society. He lives in the beautiful south hills of Eugene with his wife Maria, and children Sophia and Victor.

www.dossin.net